pond features
and decorations

pond features
and decorations

Philip Swindells

BARRON'S

First edition for the United States and Canada
published in 2002 by Barron's Educational Series, Inc.
First published in 2002 by Interpet Publishing.

All inquiries should be addressed to:

Barron's Educational Series, Inc.

250 Wireless Boulevard

Hauppauge, NY 11788

http://www.barronseduc.com

International Standard Book Number 0-7641-1845-5

Library of Congress Catalog Card Number 2001099617

THE AUTHOR

Philip Swindells is a water gardening specialist with a
long experience of growing aquatic plants in many
parts of the world. He trained at the University of
Cambridge Botanic Garden and the famous aquatic
nursery of Perrys of Enfield, and ultimately became
Curator of Harlow Carr Botanical Gardens, Harrogate.
The author of many publications on water gardening,
Philip was also formerly the editor of the *Water Garden
Journal* of the International Waterlily Society who in
1994 inducted him into their Hall of Fame. He was
awarded a Mary Hellier Scholarship in 1990 by the
International Plant Propagator's Society for pioneering
work on the propagation of water lilies.

Acknowledgments

The publishers would like to thank the
following people and companies for their much
appreciated help and advice during the
preparation of this book: "G" at Old Barn
Nurseries, Dial Post, Horsham; Hillhout Ltd for
providing decking wood and a bridge for
photography; Murrells Nursery, Pulborough,
West Sussex; and Stuart Thraves at Blagdon,
Bridgwater, Somerset.

Printed in China

9 8 7 6 5 4 3 2 1

contents

introduction 6

decks 8

lighting 10

stepping-stones 12

bridges and causeways 14

floating features 16

islands 18

edging with stone 20

edging with wood 22

natural edging with plants 24

ornaments and decorations 26

making your own deck 28

using ready-made decks 30

installing in-pool lighting 32

installing external lights 34

36 making stepping-stones

38 laying stepping-stones

40 making a wooden bridge

42 installing an arched bridge

44 making a raft for planting

46 making a wet island

48 making a dry brick island

50 edging with paving stones

52 edging with a cobble beach

54 edging with wood

56 using natural grass edging

58 edging with coir roll

60 maintaining the ecobalance

62 seasonal care

64 index

introduction

The water garden is generally regarded as a natural setting that essentially depends upon plants, fish, and a balanced ecosystem for success. This is unquestionably true, but there are many additions and improvements that can be made that can make it visually more appealing. Whether it be a bridge that permits the scene to be viewed from a different angle or lighting that extends enjoyment into the evening, the opportunities for adding extra pleasure and value to the pond should be thoroughly explored.

A water garden can be greatly enhanced by transforming it from being merely a static pond or rambling stream into a more integrated part of the garden landscape. Stepping-stones are both functional and decorative and they also change the flow and sound of the water, while a cobble beach banked up at the edge of a pond provides a convincing link to the surrounding garden, as well as a place of easy access to the water for birds and other wildlife.

Bridges and causeways offer additional ways of seeing the water, as well as the practical means of passing from one side of a feature to the other. Decks provide the perfect setting for relaxation and enjoyment of the watery scene. Pond edging is another area where decorative and functional issues coincide. Do not look at the point where the pond meets the garden as a problem area; view it

instead as an opportunity. Wood, paving stones, grass, and coir rolls can all be integrated into the water garden and provide a satisfying way of linking the pool to its surroundings.

Lighting is probably the most important addition that a water gardener can make to enhance enjoyment of the pond. Modern lighting is simple to install and available in a wide range of configurations that offer opportunities for gardens of every size. Provided that instructions are followed properly, such installations are completely safe and can transform the most modest water feature into a glittering nighttime experience. Lights are available that go in the pond to light fountains and other features, or for the poolside to throw light behind or beneath plants and statuary.

Great possibilities are offered by wet and dry islands that enable the gardener to establish a small, self-contained growing environment in the middle of an expanse of water. Planted rafts, as well as other floating features, also provide interesting ways to create interaction between hard landscaping features and the fluidity of water. With such marvelous options available, all imaginative water gardeners should look seriously at the many ways in which they can further enhance what is arguably the most attractive feature in the garden.

Above: Garden lighting can transform a water feature after dark.
Right: While water and aquatic plants are the main component of a water garden, much can be gained by introducing additional features. A bridge provides the opportunity to enjoy the pond from a different viewpoint.

decks

Decks are an extremely popular landscape feature. Pioneered in the United States, in recent years they have taken Europe by storm. Most decks are high-quality wood, but there are synthetic and often recycled materials also available. Originally wooden decks were offered as a rustic means of achieving various objectives with walkways, causeways, and sitting areas, but now it has become fashionable to paint them in all manner of interesting "designer" shades.

Right: The extensive use of decks here not only provides a neat edge to the poolside – it has become an important part of the water feature in its own right. The wood harmonizes with the water, and offers an area for poolside recreation without detracting from the importance of the pool itself.

Left: A combination of natural materials – the informality of the stones and gravel contrasts with the formality of beautifully shaped decks. Wood is a very versatile edging material, conveniently disguising what lies beneath.

Lower right: Apart from providing a neat solution to edging a water feature, a deck can also provide access, as here by means of a causeway. If carefully planned, the structure can contribute positively to the ambience of the water feature.

From the point of view of the water gardener, when a deck is suitable visually, it can provide the most useful and functional of pond edging. Not only is it a first-class disguise to conceal the ugly edge of a pond, but, when properly and sturdily constructed, it is an ideal place from which to survey and enjoy one's watery endeavors.

A deck can also be used to great effect as a causeway across a large expanse of water, or as a landing stage or a similar extension into the pool allowing the water to be appreciated from a different viewpoint.

Although rarely treated as a background for plantings, when handled in this manner a deck can be extremely effective, especially for surrounding and isolating individual plant specimens. This applies both in the water with taller marginal subjects as well as on drier land where soil conditions are more regular and stately architectural plants, such as bamboos and rhubarbs, flourish. Such plants are wonderful for the backdrop of a water garden and their foliage can soften the angular harshness of some traditional decks and assist in uniting the water feature with the rest of the garden.

lighting

It seems improbable that electrical lighting should be associated with water, but in fact it can be a harmonious partner. Not only does it highlight plants or objects located on the bank, but it can also be used within the pond as well. Modern garden lights of suitable manufacture can be placed almost anywhere within or around the pond, submerged lights being particularly effective.

Of course, electricity and water can be dangerous bedfellows, but modern wiring circuits using transformers and low-voltage cables ensure that there is no danger of personal electrocution, nor of decimating the fish population. Providing that all the manufacturer's instructions are followed, there is no reason why pond and garden lighting cannot become a permanent, safe, and most enjoyable feature of the garden landscape.

While most garden lighting draws on the electricity from the house or garage, increasingly solar energy is coming to the fore as a power source. How well this performs depends largely upon where you live and how much sunlight your garden receives, although some manufacturers have developed a system whereby recharging takes place even in cloudy conditions so lights can operate almost whatever the weather.

Below: Underwater and external lighting can transform a pond in the evening, creating a magical effect with shadows and reflections.

However, for the best and most reliable light, electricity is to be preferred. It is bright and consistent. Apart from highlighting static features, it can be used to uplight fountain sprays, not only with white light, but also with an array of contrasting colors when used with tinted lenses. These need not be static colors, for it is possible to attach a rotating disk containing several different lenses beneath a fountain jet to produce a rainbow of delight.

Left: Lighting can be used to highlight the rushing and tumbling of water. When combined with a fogger unit, turbulent rapids become an atmospheric river of fire.

Above: The most spectacular use of lighting is with a decorative fountain feature. Carefully placed uplighting can bring a touch of grandeur to a small water garden.

stepping-stones

The best way to cross a shallow band of water is by walking on stepping-stones. Not only are they visually appealing and easily installed, but they are great fun, especially for children. It almost seems as if you are walking on water.

Stepping-stones can also be used to divert the flow of water in a stream. Their presence can narrow the channel or push the water in varying directions, effectively increasing or decreasing the flow. Apart from the visual effect that this may have, the turbulence created also changes the sound of moving water.

Stepping-stones were originally natural stones that were placed in the water at strategic points to enable passage from one bank to another. Any flat-topped stones were used. This is still the most attractive and natural method of creating a crossing, although from a safety point of view each stone should have a level upper surface and be able to generously accommodate a large foot.

Choosing natural stones carefully is important; many of those derived from sandstone or limestone are so soft that they shale and disintegrate when exposed to very cold temperatures in water. The surface should also have a grip so that there is no danger of slipping; some of the granites and millstone gravels are excellent in this respect.

Nowadays garden centers are full of different kinds of manufactured stepping-stones made from both concrete and reconstituted stone. They are all excellent; the only decision to make is the choice of the shape, texture, or color that suits you best.

elow: Stepping-stones enable the garden visitor to averse the water and also to view the pond from different perspective. Although functional, stepping- ones should also ideally be decorative.

Above: Stepping-stones and paving can be used in a variety of configurations and associations with a water garden. They provide a means of crossing the water, but they also compartmentalize it and so become an integral part of the design. The use of the urn as a highlight to lift the eye, together with the careful positioning of plants with varying leaf forms, add much to this arrangement.

Left: The placement of stepping-stones need not be conventional. Their arrangement in diamond shapes and multiple groups makes a refreshing change and provides an excellent complement to the adjacent parterre hedging.

bridges and causeways

Where there is a stream, rill, or other ribbon of water in a garden, there is a natural desire to bridge it so that it can be viewed from another angle. There is also something entrancing about standing above water and viewing it from an overhead perspective. Bridges have long been the means of doing this, although across more open stretches of water or boggy ground raised causeways may be used.

Some bridges are very simple and it is their lack of an elaborate structure that gives them their charm. A plain length of stone or a single plank of wood can be functional in enabling you to cross a tiny rill or stream, but they also add visual appeal to the garden scene. Likewise, the traditional arched bridge with its minimal support enchants the eye by its simplicity.

Bridges in a garden rarely exist solely as a functional means to cross water. Indeed, in some cases water is an excuse to build a bridge that is intended to become an

Below: A highly decorative bridge is the focal point of this garden. The glassy stillness of the water allows for pleasing reflections.

Above: *A causeway permits the enjoyment of water lilies and other aquatic plants at close quarters. In addition, it provides easy access for maintenance and contributes positively to the overall aquascape.*

important focal point or garden feature. Some specially manufactured bridges are as intricate, expensive, and elaborate as the most desirable pergola or summerhouse. These are often manufactured like furniture and sold in flat packs for on-site assembly. More elaborate and expensive creations tend to come ready-made to place in position; they are best installed by a contractor.

Of course, bridges do not have to be prefabricated. Although the majority of those seen in the home garden will be of such manufacture, do-it-yourself construction from stone or brick is a further option, but not one for the novice or faint-hearted handyman.

floating features

Provided that they are suitably tethered, there are a number of floating features that can add much to the appearance of a water garden. The most impressive is the floating island. Islands are really only successful when surrounded by a reasonable expanse of water. Most aquatic enthusiasts concede that a pond measuring less than 15 x 15 ft (4.5 x 4.5 m) is unsuitable as an island will tend to crowd it out.

This is particularly so with a floating island as it is usually constructed from a standard wooden pallet. Strategically positioned empty plastic drink bottles give the raftlike structure buoyancy, and compost packages can be incorporated between the slats for planting. Such an island has to be anchored to the floor of the pond and sufficient length of rope or chain attached beneath to allow for fluctuating water levels. In a gentle breeze the raft moves around, as it may drift to the limits of its rope tether; unless the open water area it occupies is substantial, the effect can look foolish and out of place.

Other satisfying floating features include lights that float just at or slightly beneath the surface of the water. These are wonderful for lateral or submerged illumination of objects or plantings in and around the pool. They are available in a wide range of colors, but it is traditional white light that produces the most striking effects.

When the weather is appropriate, or for the indoor pool, floating candles are fun. Still conditions are desirable for their stability and to ensure a sparkling, flickering flame. Other fun effects can be created by colored balls that float across the water's surface, submerged sculptures that give a *trompe l'oeil* effect of a floating form, or even the drift across the pool of mist that is created by submerged "foggers" – small electrical devices that use sound waves to atomize water and thus create artificial fog.

Below: *The modern gardener has a wide array of floating objects available for use in the contemporary pool. Currently, decorative balls of various colors are in vogue.*

Left: *Even something as simple as a floating decoy duck can bring an extra touch of interest to a garden pool. When used in conjunction with floating plants and profuse marginal and pondside planting, the effect is very pleasing.*

Below: *Although not strictly floating, this clever portrayal of the character Bottom from Shakespeare's* A Midsummer Night's Dream *deceives the eye into believing that the head is swimming in the water. Such ornaments are unexpected and fascinating for both children and adults alike. They benefit greatly from being planted around with deepwater aquatics such as water lilies that have floating leaves and blossoms.*

islands

Islands generally look out of place in a small pond, for they also have to be small. Thus they lose much of their meaning and *raison d'être*. In addition a small island is much more difficult to construct than one of reasonable dimensions. Occasionally preformed pools offer an apology for an island in their design. Rarely are these of any great beauty, even when appropriately planted.

Even when an island is visually appropriate to a pond, its function is often not primarily a decorative one, but rather it is intended to provide a predator-free sanctuary for

Right: *Islands look best visually when surrounded by sufficient water. In most water gardens, a well-planted island such as this looks completely natural but in reality it is contrived. Where a tree or shrubs can be included, this is a great advantage, especially for the dull winter months. Here an oriental feel is conveyed by the beautifully shaped pine tree, although the peripheral plantings are in the western tradition.*

Left: *When it comes to a formal pool, an artificial island is much more in keeping. Square or circular islands that reflect the shape of the pond are most pleasing to the eye. These can also be used for some highly colored planting, especially when built as a dry island where bedding plants can be used.*

wildlife. Such an island can usually be satisfactorily accommodated in a pond with minimum dimensions of 15 x 15 ft (4.5 x 4.5 m).

The construction of islands, although wide and varied in method and material, is best carried out after the pond has been created. Unless the pond is to be a natural earth-bottomed structure sealed with bentonite clay, then much better control over the island structure can be achieved if it is added afterward.

In a pond, erosion of the island's margins is a potential problem and construction has to take this into account, while at the same time striving for as natural an appearance as possible. Few islands are appealing unless

Below right: *A contrast in styles – the peacefulness of the grass islands set off by their silver surrounds and the glassy stillness of the water is challenged by the riotous red planting in the borders and urns behind. These are built as dry islands isolated from the pond.*

planted, so suitable provision must be made for successful establishment of a variety of plants. Although an island is surrounded by water, it is possible to isolate it from this influence by the use of liner or brick walls in order to create dry conditions on the island itself. So, while the planting of "wet" islands in most cases will consist of appropriately marginal or bog garden plants, if the soil within is separated from the water by a liner, summer bedding may be more appropriate in a "dry" island.

edging with stone

The most difficult element to get right is the pond edge. Doing it correctly can certainly make the feature, while getting it wrong will ruin it completely. Whether the pond is formal or informal, the edging used is ultimately a matter of personal choice. It is certainly more usual to use paving stones for a formal feature and a stone-led planted edge for an informal one, but there are no unbreakable rules. Materials should be used that suit personal tastes and practical circumstances.

Edging is quite clearly visible and defines the pool. Wherever possible it should overhang slightly in order to protect the liner when a pond is of this construction. It should also be arranged to disguise the ungainly plastic or fiberglass edge of a preformed pond. The other important

Below: Stones and cobbles are among the most satisfactory of edges for a natural pool. Awkward edges can be easily disguised, and the use of stones as a beach is of benefit to bathing birds and wildlife.

consideration is to make the edge very stable, especially if it is an area that will be walked on.

Where stones are used as opposed to regular paving, they should be selected not only for their beauty, but also for their resistance to extreme weather. This is especially important if they come in contact with the water, for many sandstones and some limestones shale or crumble when they are saturated with water and then frozen in winter.

Although real stone is always deemed to be most desirable, nowadays there are very convincing reconstituted stone products that are easier to use. Not only are they of uniform or consistently variable shape and size, but also of a stable structure. Thus, when having to cut them to fit particular circumstances, there is little chance of them splitting and shaling in unexpected directions. Natural stones often exhibit very annoying weaknesses when it comes to cutting them.

Above: *When using stone slabs, ensure that there is an overhang at the pond edge. This disguises the area where pond meets garden and reduces the effect of sunlight on an otherwise exposed liner.*

Above right: *The use of large stones to create the effect of a mountain pool works well when there is sufficient space for bold planting. This pool combines modern pavers with ancient rocks.*

edging with wood

Wood is a natural edging, but is not always one that fits best with a natural pond, for its most common use is in providing good secure straight edges to formal features where it can be easily fastened with screws or bolts. Properly treated wood used in this fashion is inexpensive and quite long lasting, although it does not have the durability of stone.

Raw timber with its bark intact is often used to great effect out of the water in those areas where a bog or marsh garden is being established. Here it provides an informal and natural border for the bog garden or for pockets of

Below: Wood can be used in a variety of ways in the water garden, from simple edging to providing a border to a hot tub, as seen here.

planting that extend out from the pond. It is unsuitable for use beneath the water, but will serve as a water garden edging for many years, often developing its own colonies of saprophytic fungi and other interesting wild flora.

Log roll is also a useful edging, especially in a formal situation. Extensively used in many guises in the garden, from path edging to creating a raised bed, it is especially effective when used both to edge the pond and to create marginal planting areas lower down in the water.

Consisting of short lengths of prepared and treated round or half-round wood fastened with galvanized wire,

Above: *Provided that it is properly treated, wood can be used extensively in the water garden, both to edge a pond and as the main structural material, as is the case with these linked raised pools created from planks. It is best employed in formal situations and is one of the easiest materials for the practical home gardener to use.*

log roll has great flexibility of form and is capable of being arranged in both simple formal, as well as complex informal, configurations. A similar effect can be achieved with the use of short lengths of large-diameter bamboo drilled and bound with tarred rope. This creates a very special oriental effect.

natural edging with plants

While wood and stone unquestionably provide the widest range of opportunities for creating imaginative pool edging, there are other methods that are visually appealing and often more appropriate.

One of the simplest and most effective is the raised beach. Primarily used for providing access for wildlife to more natural water features, it can be used most effectively in a formal situation, especially when carefully selected cobbles of uniform color are used in association with grass or planted margins.

Grass edging is also appropriate for all kinds of ponds. It can produce a clear-cut straight edge for a formal pond or tumble over the edge into an informal feature. However, it is not without its problems when it comes to maintenance, for it is important that grass cuttings do not enter the water where they will decompose. Happily, this is not impossible to control and the resultant contrast between grass and water is worth the little extra effort that is necessary to care for the edges regularly.

Planted edges are also important, although many gardeners do not regard plants as adequate edging. This is a pity because the correct choice of plants with all the right functional qualities, which at the same time are pleasing to the eye and appropriate at the waterside, can create the most effective edging of all. They should be mat-forming species and varieties of tumbling growth, ideally evergreen or partly so, and with an ability to prosper in moist soil but at the same time not resent occasional inundation. The archetypal plant of this type is watercress.

Below: *Plants are particularly convincing when planted among poolside stones and rocks. The beautifully tended lawn running to the water's edge creates a wonderful effect.*

Left: *Plants can be used freely for edging a pond provided that the water depths are compatible. With natural plantings in an earth-bottomed pond, the edges can be defined by soil sculpting – the plants advance only as far as the water depth permits.*

Below: *Strong plantings of a single variety such as irises are essential to create a bold effect for large open spaces of water. Well-planned soil sculpting before planting will confine the irises to the desired area and their tightly knit roots will form an erosion-proof edge to the water feature.*

ornaments and decorations

The opportunities for using ornaments in a water garden are legion. Nowadays there is an industry in manufacturing everything from classical nymphs or water carriers to specially toughened mirrors or stainless steel abstract sculptures.

Beauty is in the eye of the beholder, but sometimes one has to question some of the weird wood, steel, and glass creations that are installed in modern water gardens. Provided that the pond is clear-cut and formal, such flights of the imagination can work, but for the majority of gardeners designs of a more classical nature still tend to be preferred.

Ornaments used in water gardening are often associated with the movement of water, either as items in which fountains are incorporated or linked with cascades or chutes. Often this is the best way to enjoy ornaments in a water garden setting, especially if they can be enhanced by lighting.

Ornaments should not be afterthoughts. Just as the planting has to be considered carefully in order to create an overall balance, allowing for various depths and zones, the introduction of an ornament should also be considered carefully from the outset, especially with regard to its placement.

Unlike ornaments that are used in beds, borders, or as focal points in the main garden, there is another aspect to consider when decorative objects are used in or beside water. Water in all its moods and reflectiveness can have a profound effect upon the visual character of an ornament. Whenever possible, take into account the ever-changing nature of water itself when planning how you may introduce an ornament into your waterscape.

Right: There are countless opportunities for the use of ornaments and decorations with a water garden. Here a wide combination of decorative effects is exploited, from the ornamentation within the structure of the mosaic pond itself to associated watery objects like shells and starfish, and the use of mirrors that give the impression of being windows to a garden beyond the blue wall. Water clarity is of vital importance here but it will be impossible to achieve by natural means. Water changes may be needed to keep such a feature looking good all year-round.

Left: Straight lines and clearly defined angles emphasize the simplicity of this modern water feature. Uncluttered by planting, it makes a strong statement that is highlighted by the sinuous sculpture. Decoration need not be fussy – equally pleasing effects can be achieved by a single well-placed piece like this, which provides a striking focal point.

making your own deck

As decks have become increasingly popular, it is now quite easy to purchase wood suitable for deck projects from local lumberyards or garden centers. While decks used to employ standard wood treated with a wood preservative, nowadays they are available in an array of specially manufactured configurations, usually finished to make them weatherproof. The deckboards are made with longitudinally grooved surfaces that are not only nonslip, but also visually appealing.

When it comes to making your own deck, the first and most important consideration is to purchase the best-quality wood that you can afford. Cheap wood sparingly treated with preservative not only looks bad, but will have a very limited life.

It is vital to ensure that all supports for decks are substantial; wood uprights should be at least 4 in (10 cm) square and either set in concrete or dropped into a metal fencing sleeve or pipes set into concrete. The maximum distance between structural posts should be 6 ft (180 cm). The boards themselves are mostly 6 in (15 cm) wide, although it is possible to get both narrower and wider deckboards. The gap between boards when they are fastened to the subframe should be no more than 0.2 in (5 mm); make sure that whatever gap you leave is consistent across the whole deck. The space permits the wood to move in different weather conditions and lets rainwater drain away freely. Remember to treat any sawn ends with a brand-name sealer to make them weatherproof.

Deck screws are now widely available and are the best method of securing the wood to its support, although there is still a place for bolts, especially where strong uprights require connecting. Alternatively, galvanized deck ties can be used to secure boards to the joists. The successful construction of decks depends upon careful planning and accurate measurements. But with some advance planning, it is not as complex a task as it may at first appear.

CONSTRUCTING A DECK PLATFORM

1 *The wood framework for a deck should be substantial and the individual bearers placed at intervals to provide good support. These should be set no more than 18 in (45 cm) apart, but ideally 12 in (30 cm) especially over water.*

2 *Having ensured that the framework is square and tightly secured, the first deckboard is placed in position at the desired angle. Start at one corner of the framework and work outward.*

3 *Secure the first board using deck screws. These are best screwed in using a power screwdriver. Prior to fastening it down, square off each end of this board so that it will lie flush with the frame.*

Left: *a well-constructed deck provides an ideal edge for a formal pool. Not only is it neat and pleasing to the eye, but it provides safe and easy access to the waterside for both pond maintenance and enjoyment. When installing a deck, it is important to provide strong supports and to ensure that it is level in all directions. Use only specially made deckboards and ensure that they have been pressure-treated with a wood preservative that is harmless to fish and plant life.*

4 *Position the boards so that a straight edge can be placed on them and the angle at which each has to be cut can be marked with a pencil line. Ensure a small gap between each for subsequent fixing.*

5 *The gap between boards to allow for wood movement and surface drainage need only be minimal, but it should be uniform. The end of a carpenter's pencil can be used as a convenient unit of measure.*

6 *The boards are placed in position and secured with deck screws, at least two being used at each support point. It is important to ensure that they screw vertically into the wood for a secure fit.*

7 *There is usually a small carpentry task required at the end to ensure a neat finish. It is possible to run the deck out to an even number of boards, but this rarely produces ideal overall dimensions.*

using ready-made decks

In the past decks were often overwhelmingly linear in appearance. All the boards ran in the same direction, the only concessions being made at the corners where for strength, convenience, and appearance right-angled joints were usually created.

However, with the increasing and widespread use of decks, especially in Europe and the United States, manufacturers and designers have appreciated that decks need not be simply functional, but can be an integral part of the designed landscape, making a major visual contribution to the outside living space. However, using just straight lengths of wood, the home gardener would have to be a reasonably skilled carpenter to achieve interesting patterns and variations that will have a powerful visual impact.

Realizing the limitations of the average home handyman, manufacturers have now come up with ready-made deck shapes in a series of appealing patterns and configurations. Squares are the most popular, but hexagons, octagons, circles, and other shapes are now freely available, many of which can be mixed and matched with one another. Elaborate features can be easily realized with modern deck squares.

While these can be used as part of traditional deck construction, they are also versatile enough to be attractively arranged to create landing stages and piers, the fixing arrangements being identical to those used for conventional deck construction, but with additional supports when several shapes are used together.

Left: *Ready-made decks can be used to create wonderful design effects as well as to fulfill a function in the garden. It is very important when a deck extends over the water that it has adequate support, especially when it is to be routinely used for recreational purposes, such as standing or sitting. Looking good is not enough; the structure must be safe as well.*

USING DECK SQUARES

1 *Measure and cut the support wood so that it corresponds exactly with the dimensions of the deck square.*

2 *Once cut to length, position the wood in a square and check that the deck top fits exactly. Then screw the base together.*

3 *Provide central bearers to ensure that the platform is fully supported. Once the legs are secured, these will be screwed into position.*

4 *Using deck screws and a power screwdriver, fasten the boards that form the edge of the platform to the support legs.*

5 *The whole framework can now be fastened together before the ready-made deck section is fitted on top of it.*

6 *The ready-made deck square is now ready for securing to the platform framework.*

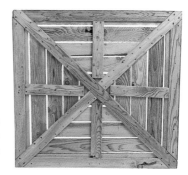

7 *Fasten the deck square using deck screws. It will fit snugly on the top of the support.*

When installed, ensure that the platform is level.

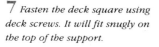

installing in-pool lighting

It is vital when installing lighting to have a very healthy respect for electricity, especially when it is in close proximity to water. Potentially this is a deadly combination. However, there should be no problem with in-pond lights providing that a reputable brand is purchased and all the instructions that are given with the equipment are adhered to properly.

Underwater lighting is quite safe – modern units are manufactured to operate with low-voltage cable and a transformer, and the light units themselves are specially sealed. For the best effect, underwater lighting can be placed beneath a fountain or waterfall feature to illuminate the tumbling water. Alternatively, it can be situated at the edge of the pool pointing inward to focus upon a particular ornament or plant grouping, or outward to illuminate an object on the pond edge. The placement of lights is not an exact science and it may be necessary to reposition the lights several times before the desired effect is achieved.

This is where floating lights can come into their own. These function in exactly the same manner as static underwater lights but are more readily adjusted to suit prevailing conditions. Along with other electrical systems, it pays to think about what effects you want to create early in the planning stages of pond construction, so that not only can lighting positions be selected, but the necessary electrical connection points can be established close at hand. Floating candles are another "low-tech" way of lighting a pond, but of course they are vulnerable to the prevailing weather conditions and likely to blow out on a windy night.

Some fountains have integral lights, which do not require any particular installation skills. However, it is important to position the fountain feature and pump on a secure flat base, and ideally in a position where the cable can be discreetly hidden as it enters the pond.

Above: *In-pool lighting can be most effective when used to highlight specific plants or pond ornaments. It is safe to use and available in a wide range of packages. Most have a transformer and white lights (right). However, the color can be changed by clipping on a different lens. Some pond lighting kits have a mechanism for attaching them to a pump; this can rotate to give several timed color changes.*

ATTACHING LIGHTS TO A FOUNTAIN

1 *One of the most effective lighting arrangements simply clips the spotlight to a pump beneath the fountainhead.*

2 *The color of the light can be changed by the use of differently colored lenses that snap on to make a watertight seal.*

3 *The submersible pump and lights are placed into position in the pool. The lights point upward beneath the fountain.*

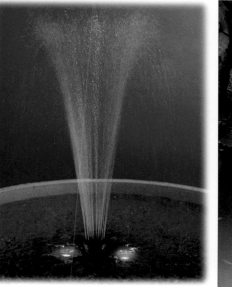

4 *When switched on, the light should illuminate all the spray pattern. Slight adjustment of the lights may be necessary.*

Right: *An underwater spotlight need not be attached to a pump. Freestanding lights can also produce dramatic effects.*

installing external lights

The majority of exterior garden lights are installed after construction of the water feature is complete. Indeed, it is often not until the pond is up and working that lighting is considered. It can then be tricky to achieve exactly the desired effect. It is better to regard lighting as an integral part of the project from the outset so that any cables and weatherproof power sockets can be carefully incorporated into the original plan.

Water and electricity are not compatible in most situations, so it is important to use only specially designed outdoor lighting and to follow installation instructions to the letter. The majority of outdoor garden lighting systems operate from a transformer that is linked to the normal domestic electrical supply. The transformer reduces the voltage to a safe level, which means that the low-voltage cables from the transformer to the light units can be run quite safely along the surface of the ground, or concealed among the surrounding plants.

This is particularly useful as it allows major adjustments to be made after the lights have been positioned and permits a certain amount of experimentation with the lighting of various garden features and plants. No underground wiring is required unless the transformer is installed in a building away from the house. The lamps can be fitted anywhere along the cable by means of a simple screw connection and are completely portable.

Once the positioning of the lights has been determined, it may be considered desirable to bury the cable so that it does not catch on a hoe or shovel while you are undertaking routine tasks. In this case use conduit to thread it through and install in a similar way to the method illustrated, which is recommended for armored cables.

MAKING IT SAFE

It is important with external lighting that every precaution is taken to guarantee safety. Waterproof connectors and plugs are essential, as is a system that uses a transformer to eliminate the risk of accidents. Follow the maker's instructions carefully.

SETTING UP EXTERNAL LIGHTS

1 *The modern garden lighting kit is safe and reliable. However, follow instructions at all times – don't be tempted to improvise.*

2 *A transformer ensures that the electrical power output into the garden is stepped down to a safe voltage.*

3 *When fixing the lights, determine the position you want them to be and then screw the connectors into the cable.*

4 *Any external cable carrying electricity should be of a waterproof armored kind and laid in a conduit inside a trench.*

5 *Plastic cable conduits have snap-on covers that keep the wire safe from any disturbance by shovel or hoe.*

6 *Once the conduit is securely positioned in the foot of the trench, cover it over with a generous layer of builder's sand.*

7 *Cover the cable with tiles for additional protection. This is a sensible precaution to protect it from future disturbance.*

8 *Stretch electrical hazard tape along the row of tiles. This gives immediate warning of danger in case it should be unearthed.*

9 *The individual lights are positioned discreetly at the poolside and focused upon carefully selected features in the pond.*

Above and right: *An entire water feature can be lit to give a dramatic appearance at night. Alternatively, waterfalls, fountains, or bridges can be selectively highlighted.*

making stepping-stones

Although a wide range of stepping-stones is available from garden centers these days, there is great satisfaction to be had from making your own. Not only is there an opportunity for originality, but stepping-stones that are produced at home are generally cheaper and will fill the gardener's requirements exactly.

The style and shape of the stones is a matter of personal taste, but size and weight do matter. The stones have to be able to be placed in position without too much man-handling and must be of a sufficient surface area to safely accommodate the larger foot and be of such a depth that they emerge above the surface of the water.

The easiest method of making stepping-stones is to use concrete made with a fine gravel and to pour this into a mold. The mold can be of lumber if the stones are to be rectangular, or of marine plywood if a more rounded shape is required. To create an interesting fluted or undulating edge, popular lawn edging materials can be cut to size and used in a box frame as illustrated to make a template for the stepping-stone.

Make the stones on a flat surface. A wooden board or similar is ideal. Do not put the mold on a concrete slab or, once cast, the stepping-stones will bond to the slab beneath. When using a wooden mold it is important to soak it thoroughly or paint the inside of the mold with a mixture of garden lime and mortar to stop the concrete from sticking.

Stepping-stones manufactured from concrete can be colored by adding colorants at the wet mix stage and, before the concrete has set, interesting stippling or textured effects can be created on the surface of the stones.

CONCRETE MIX

The ideal concrete mixture comprises four parts by volume of aggregate, two parts concreting sand, and one part cement. These are mixed together dry, water is added, and the pile is mixed again.

MAKING A CIRCULAR STEPPING-STONE

1 *Either purchase a ready-mixed dry concrete mixture or use gravel, sand, and cement. Mix it all together until of a consistent gray color. Add water gradually as mixing takes place. Do not permit the mixture to become sloppy.*

2 *The ideal mixture is of a consistent gray color and sufficiently moist that when a shovel is moved back and forth in the heap, ridges are formed that retain their character and shape.*

3 *Make a small wooden frame to match the dimensions of the proposed stepping-stone; you can create an interesting shape by using a piece of metal or plastic lawn edging.*

4 *Place the mold and frame on a piece of hardboard and then add the concrete mixture, making sure that all the indentations around the edge are filled.*

5 *Press down the concrete so that moisture exudes. This also brings some of the sand and finer aggregate to the surface for a smoother finish. The concrete will set in two days and the stepping-stone can be lifted out.*

Left: *Stepping-stones provide a convenient means of crossing water, and they are also highly decorative. While natural stones can look appealing, manufactured stepping-stones are often safer. They can also be more easily secured to a firm base.*

laying stepping-stones

The installation of stepping-stones requires some care. The positions selected should first of all be visually appealing. Stepping-stones can be an intrusion rather than an asset in a water feature when poorly placed. Of course they must also be functional and easy to traverse, at the same time being secure and level.

Stepping-stones are almost inevitably placed after construction has been completed and water added to the feature. In the case of a natural watercourse, it is difficult to assess their ideal position accurately with regard to depth unless water is flowing freely and at an average depth. However, this can create difficulties with installation, as stepping-stones are ideally placed when the water is at its lowest level. The perfect solution with a naturally variable watercourse is to take average water depth measurements and then position the stepping-stones at a time of minimal flow.

In an artificial situation this is not a problem. Water levels are either known, or if uncertain are tested, and then the stepping-stones installed appropriately. The relationship of the surface of the stones to the level of the water can be easily assessed.

Whether the installation of stepping-stones is in an artificial stream or pond, or for traversing a natural flow of water, stability is essential. The stones must be securely concreted or affixed to a level base and positioned sufficiently close to one another so that anyone crossing can do so with a normal gait. Take care to choose stones that have a naturally roughened surface – smooth surfaces are likely to become slippery when wet.

Below: *Stepping-stones are often principally for decoration. When used functionally, they must be placed at convenient even distances apart, ideally slightly closer than the length of an average stride.*

LAYING STONES ON PLINTHS

1 *A generous mortar bed must be laid to enable a level brick base for each stepping-stone to be constructed.*

2 *Start by positioning bricks in the corners. Ensure that these are set square. This base should be smaller than the stepping-stone.*

3 *Continue to lay bricks, ensuring that each is laid on an even mortar bed and is separated from the next by a layer of mortar.*

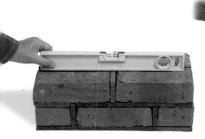

4 *Continue construction with the joints of the bricks arranged in an alternate fashion. Check regularly to ensure that they are level.*

5 *A final layer of mortar is applied when the desired height has been reached in order to secure the stepping-stone.*

6 *Place the stepping-stone gently into position on the mortar bed and firm into place. There should be a slight overhang.*

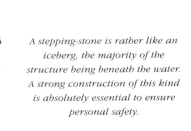

A stepping-stone is rather like an iceberg, the majority of the structure being beneath the water. A strong construction of this kind is absolutely essential to ensure personal safety.

7 *Tap the stepping-stone gently into position and make sure that it is level. Remove surplus mortar.*

making a wooden bridge

A wooden bridge or causeway provides an opportunity to see the water garden from another angle. Although they should be visually appealing, most wooden bridges are first and foremost functional; they are used rather than viewed.

Any bridge or causeway construction must have a secure foundation. This is not only necessary for the safe passage of people, but also ensures stability. Even a modest bridge can settle under its own weight if it is built with insufficient foundations. Ideally the bridge should be attached by bolts to concrete piers sunk into the ground to a depth of around 2 ft (60 cm). These are best cast in place and the bolts positioned in the concrete while it is still wet.

A causeway is really an extended bridge that takes the visitor across a large body of water, or alternatively criss-crosses a small water feature in an indirect fashion. Unlike a bridge where piers are created on either bank, a causeway is also attached to piers in the water.

The simplest method of creating supports for a causeway is to set short lengths of pipe into a concrete slab, or to bolt metal post supports to sturdy breeze blocks. The wooden supports for the bearers that will carry the planks of the causeway are dropped into these pipes after positioning in the pond. When such piers are created in a lined pool, it is important that they rest on a generous layer of fleece underlay to prevent damage to the liner.

In the creation of a wooden bridge or causeway, consider in which direction the wooden planks lie. It is an established fact that if planks are lying lengthways leading away from the bank, you are inclined to cross; if fastened crossways, you will probably linger on the bridge.

MAKING A WOODEN CAUSEWAY

1 *It is essential to have bolts firmly secured into the concrete base supports.*

2 *Bolt the metal sleeves that will hold the bridge supports securely to the base.*

3 *Put the wooden supports into the metal sleeves and make sure they are vertical.*

4 *Clamp a cross-member to each upright making sure that it is level. Use this as a template for the positioning of the other supports.*

Left: *The completed causeway – a neat and very economical method of bridging water attractively.*

5 *Secure each crosspiece with bolts in pre-drilled countersunk holes. It is imperative that all cross-members and supports align.*

6 *Drill the lengths of wood that are to form the causeway and secure them to the supports using substantial bolts.*

7 *Where there is a change in alignment of the causeway, make provision for the boards to fit neatly and evenly together.*

Above: *A causeway constructed from wood is an asset for both informal and formal water features. An offset arrangement of causeways like this breaks up the regularity of the construction, and encourages the walker to linger and admire the pool.*

installing an arched bridge

It is quite feasible to build an arched bridge from scratch, but it is more usual to purchase such a feature either ready-made or as a kit for self-assembly. When purchasing a kit or finished bridge, take care to ensure that all the dimensions are appropriate from both the practical and visual point of view. Also look carefully at the intended site before purchasing the bridge.

Even modest bridges are a considerable weight and must have sound foundations from both the point of view of safety and gradual settlement. If the soil slips, the bridge can twist and be damaged. So it is imperative that the positions of both ends of the bridge are thoroughly inspected and that suitable piers can be constructed to take the weight.

To be safe, the footings for each pier should be excavated to a depth of 2 ft (60 cm). Bridge piers can be precast, but it can be simpler in most cases to cast them in position. For most bridges, digging holes of sufficient dimensions and filling them with concrete is adequate. Take care on clay soils that shrink badly and where appropriate, include reinforcing rods in the piers.

When precast piers are used, dig the holes at least 6 in (15 cm) larger all around than the piers themselves. Place them in position and pour in concrete. Alternatively, you can build brick piers in the manner illustrated. Check that the piers on either bank are even and then install the bridge.

Right: An arched bridge is an attractive focal point in many water gardens. The subtle curving form echoes the sinuous flow of water past the planted margins.

SETTING UP A READY-MADE BRIDGE

1 *Create a level base for pier construction using mortar.*

2 *Lay bricks in an alternate arrangement to create piers.*

3 *Decide where the uprights will fit and mark the section of board that will have to be removed.*

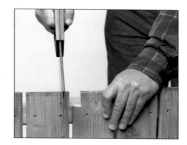

4 *Cut out the slots that will accommodate the uprights for the curved handrail.*

6 *Fasten the handrail securely. Ensure that the screws are countersunk for safety.*

7 *Drill holes through the base of the bridge to accommodate long screws. Change to a masonry drill bit when the drill reaches the bricks.*

5 *Screw the components together using rust-proof deck screws. The uprights should be evenly spaced along the bridge.*

8 *Long masonry fixings are inserted into the holes. Then the bridge is screwed securely to the brick piers.*

Above: *There are a variety of wood paints for garden features that can be used to decorate small bridges like this.*

making a raft for planting

There are a number of ways of constructing an island, but a floating feature is among the most attractive and versatile. Rather like a boat, it can be hauled to shore for maintenance. As a result of the way in which the plants are inserted into the growing medium, it is quite easy to make planting adjustments and changes when necessary.

The main part of the structure is a wooden pallet. If a full-size pallet is too large, then it is possible to reduce the size by sawing off a section. Provided that support rails are present at each side and ideally through the middle, then the pallet will remain secure and balanced. Any overhang on one side will unbalance it and tiresome adjustments will be needed to ensure level flotation.

The simplest buoyancy aids are empty plastic drink bottles. Provided that the tops are securely screwed on, they are most effective. Individually they appear as if they will make little difference, but collectively they are excellent.

The bottles are inserted into the gaps between the slats on the pallet in an even arrangement, ensuring that there is sufficient space to accommodate the growing medium. This can be put into old pantyhose, burlap squares, or sandbags and molded into the spaces that remain after the bottles have been installed. Alternatively, the whole bottom of the pallet can be covered with pond liner to make a container into which compost can be spooned, and the top of the raft covered in burlap. Young plants and rooted cuttings are then planted through slits made in the material.

Most aquatic plants flourish on a floating island, but be aware that tall or particularly leafy species do have considerable wind resistance and can drive the raft around the pool like a ship in full sail.

CREATING A PLANTED RAFT

1 *Use a wooden pallet and if necessary shorten it to the desired size. Use empty soft drink bottles pushed between the planks to provide buoyancy.*

2 *Cover the base of the pallet with pool liner, pull this taut, and then secure it with chicken wire.*

3 *Secure the liner at the sides with wood. This holds all the bottles for buoyancy firmly in position.*

4 *Provide added support beneath to take the weight of compost by adding further strengthening planks.*

5 *Add an equal mixture (by volume) of aquatic planting compost and multipurpose potting compost.*

6 *Cover the surface of the pallet tightly with burlap or sacking. Secure this at the edges of the pallet with large-headed felt nails.*

7 *Cut holes in the burlap that are large enough to accommodate the small rootballs of young aquatic plants.*

8 *Push bare-rooted plants into the compost through the holes in the burlap and water thoroughly. Cut back any that are unstable.*

9 *Complete the planting arrangement using a combination of marginal and bog garden plants, both flowering and foliage subjects.*

------ **PLANTING SUGGESTIONS** ------

Plants Used
Acorus gramineus 'Variegatus'/summer/marginal
Alisma plantago-aquatica/summer/marginal
Calla palustris/summer/marginal
Carex pendula/summer/marginal
Carex riparia 'Variegata'/summer/marginal
Cyperus hybrid/summer/marginal
Mentha aquatica/summer/marginal
Osmunda regalis/fern
Primula pulverulenta/summer/bog

Alternative Plants
Acorus calamus 'Variegatus'/summer/marginal
Butomus umbellatus/summer/marginal
Caltha palustris/spring/marginal
Matteuccia struthiopteris/fern
Primula florindae/summer/bog
Veronica beccabunga/summer/marginal

Left: *It is important to anchor the island raft to the pond floor, or it will wander around the pool driven by the wind. Attach a rope with an anchoring weight. The rope should be the same length as the depth of water if the raft is to stay in one place.*

making a wet island

One of the easiest and most effective islands to create is one built of sandbags. Such is the versatility of these malleable shapes that it is possible to achieve quite sophisticated arrangements by grouping them together, as well as ones of formal design. Sandbags are readily available from builders' suppliers and can be filled with either sand or soil as desired.

Using sand has the advantage of greater malleability and, although it is significantly heavier than soil, it does not contain nutrients that might escape into the water and create an algae problem. On the other hand, the island is never going to become a real one from the plants' point of view, for roots are not going to penetrate the sand significantly and bind the island together. Indeed, a few years down the road, if not properly maintained with a

consistent level of water, the burlap may rot, the sand spill out, and the island disintegrate.

Soil in the bags will be bound together by roots and become a solid island, but there are considerable hazards of the nutrients in the soil leaching out into the surrounding water. Even if the lower bags are filled with subsoil or clay that is relatively inert, those in the upper layers where the plants are growing will be vulnerable to nutrient escape. However, algae and slime molds will rapidly colonize the burlap and it will come to look quite natural.

The plants that will be established on sandbag islands will be bog or marginal subjects. A sandbag island is a wet island, the water table being at the level of the water in the pond that surrounds it, so marginal and bog plants will thrive in this damp habitat.

MAKING A SANDBAG ISLAND

1 *Fill sandbags with river sand. Ensure that they are all of consistent size and shape.*

2 *Arrange the sandbags rather like bricks in alternate fashion to form a solid construction.*

3 *Complete the structure so that the sandbags at the top are just at final water level.*

4 *Fill the lower part of the island where the plant roots are unlikely to penetrate, with small stones.*

5 *Top up the central part of the island with suitable compost. Aquatic planting compost is the best medium to use.*

6 *Plant toward the edge of the island using trailing plants that will hang over the side and disguise the sandbags. Space these equally around the edge.*

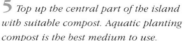

7 *Fill the center of the planting area with taller plants. Avoid invasive species that will crowd the center.*

Above: *A wet island is most appropriate for an informal pond; whether man-made or naturally occurring, it is a pleasing addition.*

8 *A tastefully planted island. Such features require replanting every second year if they are to retain their character.*

making a dry brick island

The simplest island to construct for the formal pool is one made of brick. Such construction need not be regimental and mathematical, although in practice it is easier to construct and visually most appealing if built in a square or rectangular shape. The other advantage of a brick island over any other form of construction is that it can be built as a dry island. That is one where the planting area within is drier than the marginal shelves or bog garden around the pond.

The bricks are laid in a conventional fashion to create a boxlike effect, the lower layer being laid on fleece underlay positioned on top of the liner. When the island's position is known well in advance, a solid slab or foundation can be positioned beneath the pond liner as the feature is being built to provide a secure base.

A brick island has to be relatively tall to stand above the water and this quite naturally leaves a cavernous space within. However, it does not have to be totally filled with soil or compost, although many gardeners prefer to do so. The bottom half or third can consist of small stones. If you want to make sure that the island is impermeable to seepage through the bricks, a membrane can then be placed on top of this and then brought up the sides as an inner liner.

In most cases the island can be left to its own devices, the water lapping to the top of the brickwork. However in the case of a dry island it is important that the top layer of brickwork is above water level. This can often look ugly, in which case screw a wooden plank or a deckboard to the top layer of bricks. This produces a most attractive and quite natural finish.

BUILDING A BRICK ISLAND

1 *When a brick structure is built in a lined pool, it is a wise precaution to install a support slab beneath the liner.*

2 *Lay a generous bed of mortar for the first layer of bricks and ensure that they are both square and level.*

3 *The ends of the bricks must be "buttered" with mortar to fill the gaps between them.*

4 *Lay the bricks in an alternate arrangement and ensure that each layer is level, square, and vertical.*

5 *Once the mortar has dried thoroughly, a waterproofing sealant can be applied to the inner surfaces.*

6 *Fill the lower third of the structure with small stones or gravel to provide drainage. Then top up with soil.*

7 *Choose suitable garden plants of varying flowering periods and plant as in the open garden. Here a shrub provides the focus.*

8 *A heavily planted dry island benefits from regular annual lifting and replanting.*

PLANTING SUGGESTIONS

Plants Used

Allium karataviense/summer/bulb

Armeria maritima var. *lusitanica*/
summer/herbaceous

Genista lydia/spring/shrub

Saxifraga umbrosa/spring/herbaceous

Alternative Plants

Allium 'Purple Sensation'/summer/bulb

Alyssum saxatile/spring/herbaceous

Cytisus kewensis/spring/shrub

Dianthus 'Doris'/summer/herbaceous

Above: *A dry island enables plants that are not usually associated with water to be employed in creating imaginative designs.*

Even sizeable garden trees can be included provided that they do not have root systems that will damage the island structure.

edging with paving stones

Edging with stones, slabs, and bricks looks most effective around a formal pond. Such edging can be applied to informal ponds, but it is much more difficult to create a convincing effect. With square, rectangular, and circular ponds, however, it is very attractive.

As with most other aspects of construction, it is sensible to work out the requirements for all the elements from the beginning. There is nothing more irritating than to construct a pond, only to find when the paving comes to be laid that one slab has to be cut on each side in order to finish the edging evenly, when a simple measurement before the excavation of the pond began would have resolved the problem.

Levels are also important. The pool should be level from side to side and end to end, the surrounding land having also been leveled in order to accommodate the paving. When laid, the slabs or bricks should also be level from side to side and end to end if the finished result is to be both functional and satisfying visually. Remember to leave sufficient width of liner around the margins of the pool so that the paving stones can anchor the liner securely. It is a good idea to allow for a small overhang over the edge of the pool to disguise the point where the liner overlaps the surrounding soil.

With stones, pavers, and bricks, safety is very important. A loose slab can tip an unwary visitor into the pond, so sufficient mortar of suitable strength must be used to ensure that the slabs or bricks are bedded down securely. There are also dangers with mortar of polluting the water, as escaping lime or cement can cause eye irritation in fish. So work carefully and consider using small strips of cardboard or wood as shuttering to prevent the cement used either as the foundation or as pointing from slipping into the pool until it dries and becomes hard.

PAVING PATTERNS

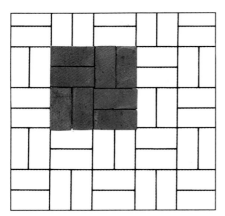

Basket Weave *One of the simplest layouts and very effective when paving of a single color is used. For a more dramatic effect, use pavers of two different colors.*

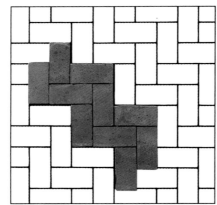

90° Herringbone *An arrangement that can be used for formal edging situations. It can look very effective with contrasting colored paving stones set around it.*

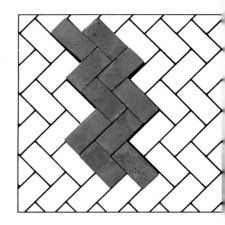

45° Herringbone *A quite complex arrangement that is best executed in paving stones of contrasting colors. It is difficult to accommodate to a pool edge.*

Left: *A formal pond is clearly defined by a paving stone edging. It is simple to create a straight edge for a square pond, but a circular one needs a little more inventiveness or the purchase of paving stones that have curved edges. These are now quite readily available.*

EDGING A POOL WITH PAVERS

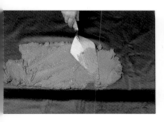

1 *Lay a generous even bed of mortar close to the edge of the pool for securing the paving.*

2 *Lay the paving stones on the mortar bed with a slight overhang. This makes the edge neat.*

3 *The second row of paving stones can be used to secure the edge of the liner in position.*

4 *Cut off any surplus liner and firm the second row of paving securely on the mortar bed.*

5 *Brush a dry mortar mix into the joints between the paving stones, taking care not to let any drop into the pond. Water gently to ensure that it will set properly.*

6 *When the edge is complete, wash off any mortar splashes. Tie the water feature to the garden landscape by using cobbles or laying dirt up to the paving stone edging.*

edging with a cobble beach

With the popularity of wildlife ponds, the cobble beach has come into its own. It is not only seen as a method of edging the pond attractively, but also as providing a ready access for wildlife, especially birds, to enjoy the watery world. It also serves as an exit for small animals that might fall into the pond, but that can then clamber to safety.

An effective method of constructing a beach is first to excavate a shallow, sloping incline at one of the margins of the pond. The liner should be stretched over this area and then secured, either by lifting the surrounding soil or turf and tucking the liner underneath, or by trapping it between two rows of bricks or stones. If the beach is not just for birds and is going to take some pressure from foot traffic, then a shallow concrete footing can be made to trap the liner. This should be continuous for the length of the beach and immovable.

Where bricks are being used, the liner should be pulled tight and secured. The area in front and behind the bricks or footing can then be covered with cobbles to create an informal look, and this arrangement of stones then extended to the water's edge. Of all the methods of edging, the beach is the cheapest and also one of the most appealing, but remember that it is not suitable for heavy foot traffic.

While cobbles are the easiest objects to use to create a beach that looks natural, there are many other materials that can be used in their place. Shells, both natural and colored, along with smooth colored glass chips or marbles can also be successfully used. Even sharp sand can be employed. However, although this looks good at first, it does tend to grow a film of algae and requires constant disturbance by brushing or raking if it is to retain its attractiveness.

Above: *A cobble and slate beach is a very neat way of finishing the edge of an informal pond. Carefully constructed, it provides easy access for wildlife to drink and bathe, and is also home to all sorts of aquatic insect life.*

CREATING A COBBLE BEACH

1 Secure the liner with turf or an edge of bricks. This is essential and provides a solid base upon which the beach is constructed.

2 It is generally advisable to lay at least two rows of bricks or stones. The liner can be trapped in place between them.

3 Once the mortar has set, cobbles can be added, the larger ones being positioned first and covering the bricks.

4 A mixture of well-washed pebbles and cobbles can then be added and heaped up to a depth of 6 to 8 in (15 to 20 cm).

5 To prevent cobbles from rolling into the bottom of the pool, create a barrier using larger stones. These will be totally submerged.

Above: A cobble beach provides a natural and easily maintained transition from lawn to pond. It is not only practical and easy to maintain but visually very appealing.

edging with wood

Wood is not as permanent a solution to edging a pond as paving, but it does have its uses. When a pond is being constructed in conjunction with a wooden deck, then wooden edging is a natural extension of the feature. It is also a good way of completing raised pools of wood construction, such as those made from railroad ties and liner. It also looks appropriate in rustic settings, even though the wood is prepared and treated formally.

There are a number of ways of fixing wood, depending upon the visual effect that it is desired. When the surface of the soil is to be even with the surrounding ground, then an innovative system must be employed with a specially constructed concrete border being built into which the wood can be bolted. The liner is trapped between this wood and wooden edging that will rest just in the water. Wooden plating joints are used to hold the two wooden sections tightly together. Their screws do not penetrate the liner and allow the water to come right to the top without seepage.

A similar system can be used with wood replacing the traditional concrete component. It will not be quite as long-lived, but will last sufficiently for most gardeners. Here it is important to use good long screws, those recommended for decks being ideal. Providing that the wooden edging is well treated with preservative it will make a durable and fine-looking edging.

Apart from the horizontal use of wooden edging, the upright log-roll type of material so frequently used for creating and edging flowerbeds can also be pressed into use using similar methods of fixing.

USING WOOD

The use of wood as an edging is ideal for the do-it-yourself enthusiast. Modern woods for garden use are now widely available already treated with a preservative. It is important for a high-quality finish to use good tools and to measure accurately.

MAKING A WOODEN BORDER

1 *A raised wooden pond can be successfully edged with wood, but protective underlay is advisable to prevent the liner from rubbing.*

2 *Pull the liner tightly over the pool edge, smoothing out the wrinkles and creating bold folds of liner to take up the slack.*

3 *Screw the wooden edging securely to the pool framework. It is advisable to use deck screws as these are rustproof.*

Above: Wood is one of the most versatile, natural, and attractive edging materials for the garden pond.

4 Cut off the surplus liner. Allow for a small overhang so that the final trimming of the liner can be concealed beneath this.

5 There are many attractive wood stains and preservatives available that are quite safe to use in close proximity to water.

6 The finished wooden edge not only secures the pond liner, but becomes an important element of the visual structure.

using natural grass edging

Grass can be a most effective natural edging and, although it does present a few minor maintenance problems, it is well worth considering in a natural setting. The important consideration with a traditional turf edging is the depth of soil required up to the edge of the pond to maintain the health of the grass.

To ensure that grass edging does not dry out, it is necessary to have a minimum depth of 2 in (5 cm) of soil, although 4 in (10 cm) is preferable. There is nothing worse than a bright green summer lawn rolling out to a water garden where the grass immediately adjacent to the pool edge is yellow or parched through lack of moisture.

If the edge is carefully arranged and the grass laid as turf, then this can be put in contact with the water that by capillary action spreads up and through the sward. It will soak up quite an amount of water during hot summer weather, so care will be needed to ensure that the pool is regularly topped up to maintain the required water level to keep the grass healthy. Where this is successful, another problem sometimes follows: vigorous uncontrolled growth, especially of grass roots that dangle down into the pond all around the margins.

This can be overcome by using a specially selected turf that will grow and prosper on rock wool. This is an inert material widely used for soil-less plant culture, and when used as a pool edging it is neat, clean cut, and very successful in containing the spread of root growth. While horticultural rock wool of a high quality is to be preferred, household rock wool used by the building industry for roof insulation has proved to be quite satisfactory also.

TURF AND ROCK WOOL EDGING

Right: Grass is a pleasing edging medium for a water garden, but it rapidly grows out of control and creates maintenance problems by invading the margins.

1 *The use of good-quality turf, especially of nonrhizomatous grasses, along with rock wool can ensure a permanently neat edge to the pond.*

2 *Lift and remove the matted roots of overgrown turf. Cut back to 12 in (30 cm) beyond the edge.*

3 *Excavate so that a section of rock wool of the dimensions of the turf can be inserted.*

4 *Ensure that the new turf can be laid on the rock wool and then water it thoroughly.*

5 *Lay the new turf on the dampened rock wool ensuring a neat edge at the poolside.*

6 *Water the turf thoroughly. You must do this regularly until the turf and rock wool knit together. This usually takes a month or more. An occasional weak liquid fertilizer is invaluable.*

7 *The rock wool will act as a sponge if in contact with the water. When the turf does not touch the water, weekly watering of the edge is advisable to maintain an attractive green sward.*

edging with coir roll

For pools that are informal and are required to take on a natural appearance, the use of coir rolls that are planted up with marginal aquatics can be recommended. Coir is a by-product of the coconut industry and is a very fibrous material with few nutrients that is ideal for plant root development and growth. By virtue of its shortage of nutrients, there is no danger of organic material leaching into the pool that would encourage the development of algae in the water. On the contrary, the coir will tend to take up nutrients as it starts slowly to decompose; the plants will also absorb their fair share and so benefit the underwater ecosystem.

Coir rolls are common in the landscape industry, coir being packed into large sausage-shaped packets wrapped with coarse rope or burlap. On a smaller scale gardeners can recreate the same or a similar effect utilizing burlap

sandbags or old pantyhose. Indeed, the rolls can be made so that they fit onto the marginal shelves exactly, coir compost from the garden center then being used as the filling.

Plants are planted through small slits made in the burlap and, if kept well watered, they will quickly establish. In spring or summer rolls can be placed out on the marginal shelves either preplanted or ready for planting. Try to keep compatible varieties of marginal aquatics in the same bag, using those that grow at similar rates to prevent the swamping of one variety by another. Once established with the planted roll pushed hard against the back of the marginal shelf, there will be a seamless transition from pool to garden, the plants leading the eye unerringly from land to water. Coir also has the benefit of not disturbing the pond's ecosystem.

PLANTING A COIR ROLL

1 *Using burlap or a sandbag, stitch and create a long sausagelike roll. This should be of a size that can be conveniently handled and will rest easily on the margin or against the pond edge.*

2 *Fill the burlap roll with finely milled coir. Unlike other organic composts, coir – a by-product of the coconut industry – contributes little to the nutrient balance and ecosystem of the pond.*

3 *Once the roll has been filled, check that it is of the correct dimensions for its intended position. Tie up the open end and then cut small planting holes into it at suitable intervals.*

4 *Use a range of non-invasive marginal plants, such as aquatic irises, for planting. Insert these bare-rooted through the holes.*

5 *Include only plants that grow at more or less the same rate.*

····· **PLANTING SUGGESTIONS** ·····

Plants Used

Carex pendula/summer/marginal
Carex riparia 'Variegata'/summer/marginal
Iris ensata 'Variegata'/summer/bog
Mentha aquatica/summer/marginal
Mimulus cardinalis/summer/bog

Alternative Plants

Butomus umbellatus/summer/marginal
Caltha palustris/spring/marginal
Iris laevigata/summer/marginal
Preslia cervina/summer/marginal
Veronica beccabunga/summer/marginal

Right: *A coir roll in which primulas have become established. The roll is hidden and the union of pond and garden is seamless.*

59

maintaining the ecobalance

A water feature is only successful if the ecosystem is in balance. There are exceptions with very small pools or fast-moving water where a natural balance of any kind is impossible to achieve, but most water features should be able to settle into a pattern of self-sustainable balance.

Where this is not practical, then chemical means usually have to be employed in order to retain water sweetness and clarity. Sometimes merely changing water will serve the purpose, but this is often difficult to undertake regularly and is usually very time-consuming.

The principles behind creating a natural balance are very clear. Submerged plants mop up nutrients in the water and provide daytime oxygen for fish and other submerged creatures. They are also coincidentally a food source for some fish and other aquatic inhabitants. By removing excess nutrients they make life difficult for the single-celled algae that otherwise turn the water green and produce a pea-soup effect. Generally the more submerged aquatics there are the better, but there should be at least ten bunches planted for each square meter (c.11 sq ft) of surface area of open water.

The presence of algae is also influenced by the amount of sunlight falling beneath the water. For submerged plants such light is vital, but it need not illuminate all the watery depths. At least a third of the surface area should be shaded by floating aquatics or the leaves of water lilies and other deep-water aquatics. Other forms of shade, such as that cast by a building or trees, are not quite the same and bring their own problems, particularly general poor growth of other aquatics as well as those of leaf accumulation when trees are used.

Marginal aquatics brighten up the water feature, but make little difference to the water garden ecosystem. Where the foliage or flowers are especially attractive to wildlife, then this is an added bonus. Likewise, fish are useful in that they control aquatic insect pests, but for the most part they are purely decorative and should be introduced sparingly.

Moving water can also be embraced by a balanced eco-system, but the introduction of floating plants is not practical when water is flowing, and the establishment of water lilies and several other deepwater aquatic species is difficult as they resent moving water, so providing shade to the surface of the water is not so easy. However, the introduction of simple natural or biological filtration can resolve this problem another way.

POND MAINTENANCE

Above: It is important to remove algae regularly. On cobble beaches, the only successful method of control is by hand.

Below: Aquatic snail species with pointed shells cause damage to water plants. They should be caught and removed, if possible.

Above: Submerged plants are necessary to ensure a good ecobalance in a pool. They must be thinned if they grow too profuse.

Below: *With the careful use of submerged aquatics and both floating and deep-water plants, a naturally sustaining balance can be successfully achieved.*

seasonal care

The spring is the best time for establishing plants and introducing fish to a pond or water feature. There are one or two very early flowering aquatic species, notably among the marsh marigolds, and these are best planted immediately flowering is over unless established in a container. When spring planting is not possible, then summer establishment can be undertaken. All aquatic plants happily transplant at that time, but often have to be cut back in order to establish properly, thereby ruining their period of floral beauty for that season.

Spring is traditionally propagation time, and apart from conventional division, water lilies can be increased from "eyes" and water forget-me-nots and mimulus (monkey flowers) from seed. The cuttings of plants like watercress and watermint are best rooted during early summer when the flush of early growth subsides.

Fish can be introduced to the pond at any time during spring or summer. When introducing new fish it is a wise precaution to dip them in methylene blue to disinfect them against maladies such as fungus and fin rot. These

CLEANING LIGHTS

Right: *Periodically, underwater lights require removing from the pond and cleaning. They are of a shape that seems to attract blanket weed and silkweed to cling to them. In order to ensure the best-quality light, the lenses require regular attention. A stiff brush is the best way of returning them to a pristine condition.*

Left: *To maintain this attractive pond in good order requires regular care. Attention for half an hour each week will keep it looking good all year-round. Topping up with water to compensate for evaporation must be undertaken regularly.*

Above and above right: *Although one of the most attractive floating plants, fairy moss (*Azolla caroliniana*) can get out of control and smother other plants. Removal with a net is the only solution.*

diseases spread quickly, especially in a well-balanced pond where there are healthy fish. Never place new introductions into a pond until disinfection has taken place or you risk the health of your existing stock.

During the summer it is very much a matter of keeping on top of blanket weed whenever it appears, twisting it out with a stick. Aquatic plants should be regularly manicured, fading blossoms and foliage being removed, and when necessary dense floating subjects, such as fairy moss, rationalized. Submerged plants can be thinned, but very cautiously as removing too many will disrupt the natural balance of the pond.

As fall arrives the pump should be removed, cleaned, and put into storage to be replaced by a pool heater. The same goes for other submerged equipment, such as in-pool lights and fountainheads. Net the pond or its borders to prevent leaves accumulating in the water, as when they decompose they produce noxious gases that in an ice-covered pond are dangerous for fish. Never transplant aquatic plants in the fall; it is only true bog plants that can be moved safely in their dormant state. Fall is a good time to scrub surfaces that are walked on, such as decks, bridges, stepping-stones, and pond edges, to remove any

accumulated slime that might make them slippery and unsafe.

Winter care of a water feature is minimal. If water freezes over and there are fish present, then ensure that the ice is vented to allow for the exchange of air. Do not hit the ice to break it – this creates shock waves that can concuss the fish. Instead, boil some water in a pan, then stand the hot pan on the ice and allow it to melt through. This creates a hole in the ice through which gases can permeate. All popular aquatic plants are completely hardy and will come to no harm during winter.

Above: *At the approach of winter and again in spring, it is important to scrub decks in order to remove encrusted algae and other debris. A stiff brush and soapy water is an effective treatment.*

index

Note: *Italic numbers
indicate references to
photo captions*

algae 46, 52, 60, *60*, 63

balls, floating 16, *17*
beaches
    cobbled 6, 24, 52-53, *52,
    53*
    raised 24
blanket weed 63
bricks *39, 43,* 48-49, *48, 49,*
    52, *53*
bridges *6,* 14-15, *14, 35,* 63
    arched 42-43, *42*
    clapper 14
    installing 42-43, *43*
    making 40
    prefabricated 15, 42-43
    wooden 40-41
burlap 44, *44, 45,* 46, *58*

candles, floating 16, 32
cascades 26
causeways 6, 8, *8,* 14-15,
    15, 40, *41*
    making 40-41, *40, 41*
chutes 26
cobbles 6, *20,* 24, *51,* 52, *53*

coir *see* edging, coir
compost *44, 45, 46,* 48
concrete 36, *36,* 54

decking 6, 8-9, *8,* 48, 54, 63
    construction 28-29, *28,
    29*
    ready-made 30-31, *30, 31*

ecosystem 58, 60
edging 6, 8
    bamboo 23
    coir 6, 58-59, *58, 59*
    grass 6, 24, *25,* 56-57, *57*
    log roll 23, 54
    paved 50-51, *51*
    planted 24-25, *25*
    stone 6, 20-21
electricity 10, 32, *32,* 34
erosion 18, *25*

filtration units 60
fish 60, 62, 63
fogger units *11,* 16
fountains 6, 11, *11,* 26, 32,
    33, 35, 63

islands 6, 18-19, *18,* 44
    construction 18, 46-47,
    46, 47, 48-49, *49*

"dry" *18,* 19, *19,* 48-49
floating 16
"wet" 19, 46-47, *47*

landing stages 30
lighting 6, *6,* 10-11, 26
    color 11, *32, 33*
    floating 16, 32
    in-pond 32-33, *32,* 63
    installation 32-33, 34-35
    solar 10
    underwater *10, 33, 62*
    uplighting 11, *11*
liner 19, 20, *21, 44,* 52, *53,*
    54, *54, 55*
log roll 23, 54

mirrors 26, *27*

ornaments 26-27, 32, *32*

paints 8, 43
paving stones *13,* 20, 21,
    21, 50-51, *50*
piers 30, 42, *43*
plants 6, *15,* 18, 44, *45, 47,*
    49, *49,* 62, 63
    bog 19, *45,* 46, *59,* 63
    deep-water *17,* 60, *61*
    floating *17,* 60, *61*

marginal 9, *17,* 23, *44,
    45, 46, 47,* 58, *59,* 60
    pondside *17*
    submerged 60, *60, 61*
pools
    preformed 18, 20
    raised 54
preservatives, wood *55*
pumps 63

rafts, planted 6, 16, 44-45
rock wool 56, *56,* 57

sandbags 44, 46, *46,* 58,
    58
sculptures 16, *17,* 26, *27*
snails *60*
stepping-stones 6, 12-13,
    13, 36-37, *37, 38,* 63
    laying 38-39
    making 36-37, *36, 37*
stone slabs *20, 21,* 50
streams 6, 12, 38

timber, *see* wood

waterfalls 32, *35*
wood 6, 8, 22-23, *22, 23,*
    54-55, *54, 55*
wood stains *55*

Photo Credits
Eric Crichton Photos: 3 (design: Mark Davis, RHS Hampton Court 2001), 4 (Mrs. Una Carr, (NGS) Avon), 8-9 (design: S. Rendell & J. Tavender, Dorset Water Lily Co, RHS Hampton Court 2001), 9 (RHS Chelsea 1997), 12-13 (Wyevale Garden Centres, RHS Chelsea 1997), 18 (Mitsubishi Garden, RHS Hampton Court 2001), 20 (design: Mamey Hall, RHS Hampton Court 2001), 21 left, 24-25 (design: Crockett and Summers, Dorset Water Lily Co, RHS Hampton Court 1999), 26 (design: Charles Funk, Evening Standard, RHS Chelsea 2001), 29 (as 8-9), 37 (The Quarryman Garden, RHS Chelsea 1998), 49 (design: Arabella Lennox-Boyd, Evening Standard, RHS Chelsea 2000), 51 ("Country Living", RHS Chelsea 1993), 55, 59, 61 (design: Daniel Lloyd-Morgan, Anglo Aquarium Plant Co, RHS Hampton Court 2001). **John Glover:** 13 bottom, 16-17, 17 top, 25 top, 47. **Jerry Harpur:** 6 (Villa Bebek Bali), 13 top (design: David Stevens, RHS Chelsea 1993), 23 (Susanna Brown and Catalyst TV). **Marcus Harpur:** 11 left (London Borough of Barnet, RHS Chelsea 2001), 52 (Paul Dyer, RHS Hampton Court 2001). **S. and O. Mathews:** 18-19, 21 right, 38. **Clive Nichols Garden Pictures:** 7 (Leyhill Prison, RHS Chelsea 2000), 10 (Garden & Security Lighting), 11 right (Garden & Security Lighting), 14, 22, 25 bottom (Brook Cottage, Oxon), 27 (design: Ann Firth), 33 (Garden & Security Lighting), 35 (Garden & Security Lighting), 41 (Architectural Plants, Sussex), 42 (Little Coopers, Hampshire), 57 (Mr Fraser/design: Julian Treyer-Evans), 62 (Vale End, Surrey). **Neil Sutherland:** 1, 5, 8, 15, 17 bottom, 19, 30.